JARROLD SHORT WALKS

N
S
coastal fringe

Compiled by
Dennis and Jan Kelsall

ARROLD
publishing

Mapping
sourced from

Ordnance
Survey

Text: Dennis and Jan Kelsall
Photography: Dennis Kelsall
Editorial: Ark Creative, Norwich
Design: Ark Creative, Norwich

© Jarrold Publishing 2005

 This product includes mapping data licensed from Ordnance Survey® with the permission of the Controller of Her Majesty's Stationery Office. © Crown Copyright 2005. All rights reserved. Licence number 100017593. Ordnance Survey, the OS symbol and Pathfinder are registered trademarks and Explorer, Landranger and Outdoor Leisure are trademarks of the Ordnance Survey, the national mapping agency of Great Britain.

Jarrold Publishing
ISBN 0-7117-3859-9

While every care has been taken to ensure the accuracy of the route directions, the publishers cannot accept responsibility for errors or omissions, or for changes in details given. The countryside is not static: hedges and fences can be removed, field boundaries can alter, footpaths can be rerouted and changes in ownership can result in the closure or diversion of some concessionary paths. Also, paths that are easy and pleasant for walking in fine conditions may become slippery, muddy and difficult in wet weather, while stepping stones across rivers and streams may become impassable.

If you find an inaccuracy in either the text or maps, please write to or e-mail Jarrold Publishing at the addresses below.

First published 2005
by Jarrold Publishing

Printed in Belgium
by Proost NV, Turnhout. 1/05

Jarrold Publishing
Pathfinder Guides, Whitefriars,
Norwich NR3 1TR
email: info@totalwalking.co.uk
www.totalwalking.co.uk

Front cover: A boat on Thorpeness beach
Previous page: Brograve Drainage Mill beside Waxham New Cut

Contents

Keymap

Introduction

First time visitors to the coastal areas of Norfolk and Suffolk may be surprised at the landscape they encounter, for although there are vast areas of low-lying ground, it is not the monotonous dead flat expanse that some imagine. Set against a backdrop of gently rolling countryside that is broken by rich woodlands, undulating heaths, winding tracts of water and picturesque villages, is an intriguing fringe that is precariously balanced in an age-old contest between man and the sea. In places embankments, dunes and sea walls mark an impermanent boundary where the water has been pushed back from the land. Elsewhere however, nature's barrier of low cliffs succumbs to relentlessly pounding waves and, in places, up to two miles (3.2km) have been claimed by the sea over the last 2,000 years. Equally vulnerable is the land surrounding the meandering tentacles of water that snake inland from the east called the Broads, for that too has been wrested from the surge and fall of the North Sea tides.

Sea defences

Before the Romans arrived, much of the coastal region was a wilderness of marsh, saltings and dunes, broken by a maze of twisting creeks and inlets that marked the mouths of languid rivers and streams. Standing out as islands and low peninsulas were areas of higher ground, which offered secure places to live for the small communities fringing the kingdom of the Iceni, the British tribe that held this corner of the country. Whilst Bronze and Iron Age farmers may have begun to change the face of the countryside by clearing tracts of the all-pervading forests, it was the Romans who made the first attempts to master the water, digging drainage ditches and improving the course of rivers to render them navigable. Apart from the Bishop of Ely's efforts to train the River Nene in the Middle Ages, little subsequently happened until the 1630s when a Dutch engineer named Cornelius Vermuyden was commissioned to begin draining the marshes above King's Lynn. His work was considerable and produced a 21-mile (33.8km) cut that runs near straight between Earith and Denver. Its success paved the way for even more expansionist plans and the 18th century saw the construction of miles of coastal

Sailing a wherry along the River Burgh

embankments and an intricate network of ditches, channels and river straightenings. As much of the newly created land was below the level of the sea, windpumps and sluices sprang up everywhere to lift and usher the water away to the coast.

The massive effort brought losers and winners. Many villages that during the Middle Ages had been thriving ports were now stranded inland, but that was perhaps a small price to pay against a level of security from inundation. However, the battle against the sea is a constant fight and it is held at bay only by constant pumping, the careful management of the watercourses and continual maintenance of the sea defences. Despite all this, there have been floods in living memory as equally devastating as those of long ago. Winter storms are not the only problem; the gradual downward tilt of Britain's east coast is being compounded by rising sea levels resulting from global warming. Ultimately, the cards are stacked in Nature's favour, but nothing will be given up easily.

A natural haven

Yet, despite its impermanence and fragility, the seaward face of Norfolk and Suffolk contains some of the most important wildlife areas in the country and has a singular haunting beauty that is unmatched anywhere

A pool on Dunwich Heath

Cottages in Blythburgh

else. This is recognised in much of it being included within areas of protection; the Broads as a unique National Park, and much of the coast within a succession of nature reserves and two Areas of Outstanding Natural Beauty. The term 'natural' here seems odd, because in reality they are perhaps the most intensively man-managed in the whole country. Centuries of medieval peat cutting (which flooded to create the Broads), grazing, drainage and protection schemes have created a landscape that is endlessly varied, ranging through sandy heather and grass heathland (one of the rarest wildlife environments in the country), wet and dry woodland, and marshland grazing to fresh and salt-water pools, creeks, dunes and mudflats. These differing habitats are often laid side by side and, because nothing is static, often only a fine balance separates the one from another. Each attracts their own spectrum of plants, birds and animals; the flora changing with the seasons and many species of birds making an appearance at certain times of the year. Consequently there is always something new and often unexpected to see and a relatively short walk can lead you through two or three completely different environments.

For bird watchers, the area must seem a complete paradise, with endless miles of mudflats, saltings, grazing marshes and pools attracting a succession of birds throughout the year. Along the coast are some of Britain's most important bird reserves such as the Cley Marshes (Norfolk Wildlife Trust) and Minsmere (RSPB), whilst Hickling Broad (also

Holiday chalets at Heacham

Norfolk Wildlife Trust) lies a little inland, the largest area of lake amongst the intricate waterways of the Broads. There are many breeding species, including some of the country's rarest birds such as marsh harriers, bitterns and bearded reedlings, whilst spring and autumn see passing migrants en route to and from the Arctic and Africa. Winter is marked by the arrival of flocks of ducks, geese and waders, which feed in their thousands upon the mudflats and grazing meadows. Plant and flower lovers will also find much to explore amongst the contrasting habitats of salt marsh, dunes, woodlands and heaths. Spring and autumn are particularly rewarding times. Masses of flowers carpet the woods and hedgerows from early in the year into summer, whilst the golden tints of turning leaves and strange fungi sprouting amongst the dying litter provide a different focus as the days start to draw in. There is also much to delight those with more general interests; in the windpumps and mills, stately houses, churches and charming villages of flint cottages that dot the countryside. The fresh breezes sweeping off the sea lend a clarity to the vast skies above the low-lying countryside, giving the expansive landscapes a vividness that is sometimes unreal, an unbridled inspiration to artists and photographers.

Meandering walks

For the most part uncrowded, the area is a place of quiet retreats, where it is easy to slip out of the frantic pressures of a work-a-day life. With no significant hills, the walking is never demanding and invites a leisurely approach to the day. These routes explore the variety of subtly changing moods and characters of the coast and hinterland, contrasting rich natural woodland with wild open saltings and lonely undulating heaths with the twisting waterways of the Broads. From the top of Beacon Hill, which at 340ft (104m) is Norfolk's highest summit but barely one mile

Deep in a wetland wood

(1.6km) from the coast, to reed beds beside winding rivers, barely above sea level yet 20 meandering miles (32km) from the coast, there is something here for everyone.

Along the dunes at Snettisham Coastal Nature Reserve

1 *Castle Rising*

START Castle Rising (grid ref: TF 666244)

DISTANCE 2¼ miles (3.6km)

TIME 1 hour

PARKING Visitors exploring the castle or village may use the castle car park, but should note that it is locked when the castle closes

ROUTE FEATURES Field tracks and woodland paths

Overlooking the vast expanse that was once the tidal estuary of the River Babingley, Castle Rising is a dramatic example of early Norman military architecture and well worth exploring. From it, this undemanding walk takes you through the picturesque village with its ancient church and 17th-century almshouses, Trinity Hospital, to the lazily flowing river, returning by way of pleasant woodlands and gently undulating fields.

Trinity Hospital almshouses

🖉 From the castle car park, walk past the ticket office and castle entrance to a lane at the bottom and follow it left to a crossroads in the village. Turning right, wind by the Black Horse Inn to the next junction, and there go ahead along a cul-de-sac between the church and almshouses.

When you reach a gate at the end, a disused road curves around the northern edge of Castle Rising Wood, the open fields extending a view across the reclaimed marshes

PUBLIC TRANSPORT Bus service to village

REFRESHMENTS Tearoom café at post office and Black Horse Inn, both in Castle Rising

PUBLIC TOILETS Adjacent to castle car park

ORDNANCE SURVEY MAPS Explorer 250 (Norfolk Coast West)

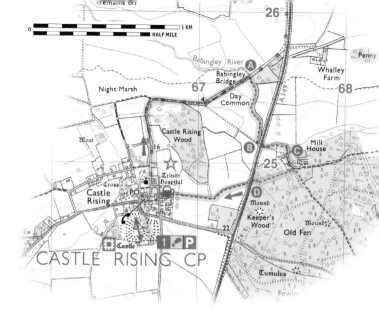

At one time, the tide rose along the river as far as the village and, throughout the medieval period, **Castle Rising** prospered as a busy port. Founded in 1138 by William de Albini, the spacious keep is set within a massive encircling earthwork that in its day must have seemed all but impregnable. The **castle** has been home to the widows of two English kings; Adelaide of Louvain, who married William after the death of Henry I, and then Isabella, formerly the wife of Edward II. The castle was later furnished as a hunting lodge by her grandson, the Black Prince and eventually passed to the Howard family, who have held it since 1544.

to the lonely ruins of St Felix's Church. You can reach the building after the walk from a track

signposted off the main road, to the north of the village at Babingley. For the time being however, carry on along the track to Babingley Bridge **A**.

Instead of crossing this, turn off onto a riverside path on the right, which winds upstream at the edge of Day Common. In spring and summer, the overgrown margins of the water are well spotted with flowers and the fronds growing from the riverbed wave gently in the current. The path ends at the main A149 road **B** and, *as it is often busy with quickly moving traffic, be careful as you cross to a footpath on the other side.*

Castle Rising Castle

A sign points the way over a stile into a small field. Carry on beside the riverbank, passing a gnarled beech tree to find another stile in the corner. A path to the right then follows the edge of a small copse, coming out at its far end onto a junction of tracks **C**.

Taking the one opposite, walk to a left-hand bend. Go right and immediately right again beside a leylandii hedge. Beyond its end, the path continues into a wood of birch, oak and pine, winding on across a stream. At the far side of the trees, look for a plank bridge spanning a drainage ditch,

? *How many cat's faces are carved on the font to be found in St Lawrence's Church?*

emerging beyond it onto the main road **D**. *Again, exercise caution as you cross to a track*, which leads away between cultivated fields. Cresting a gentle rise it then drops to follow a hedge towards Castle Rising, whose buildings now appear amongst the trees ahead. Beyond the fields, keep going on an enclosed path between cottage gardens to reach a lane. Turn right and follow it back into the centre of the village.

Beacon Hill

START Car park off Sandy
Lane, West Runton
(grid ref: TG 183414)
DISTANCE 2¼ miles
(3.6km)
TIME 1 hour
PARKING National Trust
car park (Pay and Display,
NT members free)
ROUTE FEATURES
Woodland tracks and
paths

2

*Romantically carrying the title 'Roman
Camp', Beacon Hill is the highest spot in
the whole of Norfolk and offers some
splendid panoramas to the coast from its
wooded slopes. The route drops below the
northern flank of the hill, climbing to a
second viewpoint at the other end of the
ridge before meandering back through
the trees.*

Beginning from the car park
opposite the entrance to a small
caravan site, head across the grass
past a flagpole to a viewpoint, from
which the land falls sharply
towards the coast. A path to the
left of a bench drops steeply into
woodland, where sweet chestnut,
beech, holly and oak grow in
abundance. Levelling in a partial
clearing at the bottom, the way
reaches the boundary of the
National Trust property Ⓐ.

Swing left through a barrier to
follow a path inside the fence,
which undulates behind a

succession of house gardens.
Ignore minor trails off into the
trees, and later, a joining waymarked
path, to reach a prominent fork.
Bear left to remain within the
perimeter of the wood, shortly
arriving at another junction beside
a small pond, which lies over on
the right half-hidden by the
foliage Ⓑ.

Go right and then almost
immediately left onto Calves Well
Lane, a sandy track that fringes the
wood above grass fields. The
flowers sprouting underneath the
bounding hedge are a delight in

PUBLIC TRANSPORT None
REFRESHMENTS None
PUBLIC TOILETS None
ORDNANCE SURVEY MAPS Explorer 252 (Norfolk Coast East)

Woodland path beneath Beacon Hill

spring, whilst occasional gaps proffer views across the parish of Beeston. Before long, the Peddars Way and Norfolk Coast Path joins from the left, leaving again at a crossing a little farther on. The route, however, keeps ahead at this point, very soon approaching a cottage nestling at the edge of the

Although only a mile (1.6km) from the coast, **Beacon Hill** rises to 340ft (104m) and is **the highest point in the county of Norfolk.** With an all-round prospect, it would have been a perfect site for an ancient fortification, and the many low embankments and ditches crowding its summit ridge prompted imaginative Victorians to dub the place 'Roman Camp'. However, although there is no evidence of any such settlement, the Anglo-Saxons were certainly busy up here mining for iron ore.

View to the coast from the foot of Beacon Hill

trees. Bypass it to the right along a broad swathe of grass **C**.

Carry on along a narrower trail, passing a grass path and then shortly coming to a marked bridleway leaving on the left. It swings away, gaining height along a small valley that is crowded with oak, before breaking out higher up onto more open heath. As the way levels, look for a junction where a path strikes off to the right, paralleling the tree line along the ridge of the hill. It leads to a viewpoint on the top of Stone Hill, where a topograph beside a bench

? *Two square-towered churches are visible from the viewpoint on Stone Hill, which are they?*

indicates some of the local landmarks **D**.

Retrace your steps to the last junction and now go right, entering the trees to find a lateral fence. Turn left beside it, very soon reaching the corner at a crossing of paths. Bearing slightly right walk on a few paces to a second junction and keep forward on a straight path that falls gently through the wood. Meeting a broader path, follow it left for about ⅓ mile (500m), again ignoring successive paths leaving on either side. The track eventually curves left to meet a dirt track **E**. Turn right. At a later junction, go left and then immediately right onto a firmer drive, which runs for ⅓ mile (500m) back to the parking area. ●

3 *Felbrigg*

START Felbrigg Hall
(grid ref: TG 194394)
DISTANCE 2¾ miles
(4.4km)
TIME 1¼ hours
PARKING National Trust
car park
ROUTE FEATURES
Woodland paths and
drives

*Norfolk has no shortage of impressive
country homes, many of which are open to
the public. Felbrigg is amongst the most
elegant, a grand 17th-century house full of
character and life, lent by contents and
furnishings that remain from the time
when it was a family home. This easy walk explores
something of the extensive park surrounding it, crossing
open fields to an ornamental lake before returning through
the magnificent trees of Great Wood.*

A signpost by the information
panel beside the path to the visitor
entrance of the house points the
way left to Felbrigg Church.
Leaving the car park through a
gate, follow an obvious field track
that curves across parkland grazing
towards a square-towered church,
sitting alone within the walled
enclosure of its graveyard **Ⓐ**.

Walk past the churchyard to a field
gate, through which, cut a right
diagonal across the field. Go
beneath a couple of massive beech
trees into the corner where you

Until the middle of the 16th
century, the village of Felbrigg
clustered around its parish church, **St
Margaret's**, but was abandoned, it is
thought, after a disastrous visitation
of plague in 1549 when the villagers
moved ½ mile (800m) to the north
east to escape the pestilence. The
many fine **brasses** in the church
depicting members of the de Felbrigg
and Windham families span some
500 years and offer a fascinating
insight into the changing styles of
dress over the period.

will find a small gate tucked away
on the right. Entering the next
field, walk down beside a flint and

PUBLIC TRANSPORT None
REFRESHMENTS Tearoom and restaurant in stables
PUBLIC TOILETS In stables
PICNIC/PLAY AREA Picnic area by car park
ORDNANCE SURVEY MAPS Explorer 252 (Norfolk Coast East)

Near Felbrigg Hall

brick wall towards the foot of Felbrigg Pond **B**.

Emerging onto a grassy strip, keep going across the low dam to a track climbing away at the far side. Almost immediately, turn off right into the trees to find a lakeside path. It soon moves away from the water along a wooden footway over marsh, later passing through a gate into more open ground. The way curves in a gentle arc around a rough meadow to another gate through which, a contained path dips across the shallow valley at the head of the pool **C**.

Reaching the higher ground beyond, it turns abruptly left, passing the massive bole of an

Once part of a vast Norman estate held by Roger Bigood, the manor passed to one of his lesser descendants in the 13th century who adopted its name as his own, de Felbrigg. Parts of the original house can still be found in the basement of the **present Felbrigg Hall**, whose magnificent mullion-windowed southern wing was begun in the early 1620s by Thomas Windham. His family had bought the estate some 170 years earlier, and retained it more or less, until it was bequeathed to the National Trust on the death of Robert Wyndham Ketton-Cremer in 1969.

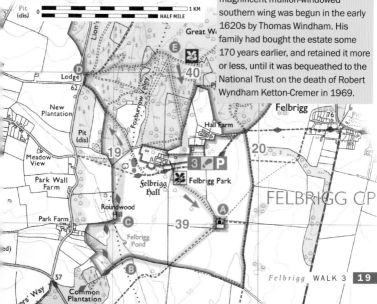

ancient oak. Entering woodland at the far end, bend around to the right and walk through to meet the estate drive beside a cattle-grid. To the left, it eventually leads to a lodge at the edge of the park **D**.

Turn off immediately before the lodge onto a gravel path on the right. Gently gaining height, it meanders through a rich woodland tapestry of sweet chestnut, oak, beech and larch, each contributing their individual texture and colour to the picture. Towards the top of the rise, half-hidden by the vegetation on the right, is the entrance to an ice house. Ice, cut from the lake in winter was stored inside and then taken out in pieces

? *When was the 'Victory V' planted?*

as required through the following year for use at the big house. Beyond there, the gradient eases and the path swings to the right, conducting you to a bench overlooking two broad beech avenues that rise to a point at the top of the hill **E**.

Bearing right, descend along the second of the rides, emerging through a gate at the bottom of the wood. Keep ahead along a paddock past the entrance to the walled gardens, finally returning to the car park just a little farther on. ●

Felbrigg Hall

● Woodland landscape ● gazebo ● folly

Sheringham Park

4

START Sheringham Park Visitor Centre (grid ref: TG 139411)	
DISTANCE 3 miles (4.8km)	
TIME 1¼ hours	
PARKING National Trust car park (Pay and Display, NT members free)	
ROUTE FEATURES Woodland tracks and paths	

High ground replaces the fringing marshland in this north-eastern corner of Norfolk, and offers fine prospects over the surrounding landscape. This enjoyable walk wanders through the National Trust's Sheringham estate to a hill top gazebo, from which there is a splendid view to the coast. Below runs the North Norfolk Railway, along which steam trains regularly puff nostalgically across the countryside.

Panoramic view from the gazebo

🥾 Leaving the car park, walk past the visitor centre onto the main drive, following it left to join a metalled path into the woodland **A**. Ignore a boardwalk and

subsequent side paths to gently wind through the trees, some of which were planted almost two centuries ago. Lofty pines, majestic oaks and imposing beech tower above rhododendrons and azaleas, whose colourful blooms provide a splendid show during late spring and early summer.

Undulating downwards, the way later curves around at the western side of the park before breaking from the trees across open grazing land **B**. Sheringham Hall, which is not open to the public, lies ahead

PUBLIC TRANSPORT None
REFRESHMENTS Snack bar at visitor centre
PUBLIC TOILETS At visitor centre
PICNIC/PLAY AREA Picnic site adjacent to visitor centre
ORDNANCE SURVEY MAPS Explorer 252 (Norfolk Coast East)

at the foot of an oak-clad hill, whilst over to the right on a grassy hillock stands an eye-catching ornamental temple, which is visited later on during the walk.

For the time being, remain with the drive across a cattle-grid, soon reaching a junction near the hall. Turn left off the tarmac onto a grass track signed to the gazebo and walk down to a gate at the edge of the park. Turn right along the field perimeter beside a wood, the path to the viewpoint leading into it just a little farther along **C**. It climbs purposefully to the summit of the hill, but as closely packed oaks obscure the view, you must carry on to the top of the gazebo's staircase to peer out over the leafy tree-tops.

Sheringham Park was laid out in the early part of the 19th century for the Upcher family to a design produced by one of the leading landscape gardeners of the day, Humphry Repton. Repton often collaborated with his architect son, John Adey, and he designed Sheringham Hall. The **temple folly** was erected in 1976 to mark the 70th birthday of Thomas Upcher, the last of the family to live here. It is based on an idea put forward by John Adey, but was never realised at the time.

The gazebo

? *How many steps is it to the top of the gazebo?*

As you retrace your steps down the hill to point **C** decide whether you want to extend the walk to the coast. *If so, go right, following the edge of the wood to the main road, where on the other side, a little to the right, a track continues between the fields and over the railway to the sea.* The trek there and back adds a little less than two miles

(3.2km) to the walk.

Otherwise, turn left and walk back to the junction by the hall, now continuing forward along the main drive. Carry on past an estate lodge and then Hall Farm, which lies over to the left, going as far as the last of the farm's buildings. There, leave the drive and climb along a mown swathe to the temple folly **D**, perfectly sited for a fine view across the park to the hall, almost ½ mile (800m) away.

Walk past the columned pile to a gate behind, passing through the trees beyond to a second gate. Maintain the same line across the corner of a sloping meadow, re-entering Sheringham Wood at the bottom. A path to the left twists steeply up through the trees to a boardwalk that leads along a narrow ridge of high ground. Beyond a break in the trees that gives a striking glimpse into the narrow valley, regain the metalled path. Turn left and retrace your outward steps along it back to the visitor centre and car park. ●

Royal residence ● gardens ● woodland country park

5 *Sandringham*

START Sandringham
Country Park Visitor Centre
(grid ref: TF 689287)
DISTANCE 3 miles (4.8km)
TIME 1¼ hours
PARKING Free car park
near visitor centre
ROUTE FEATURES Woodland
paths and tracks

Sandringham House lies at the heart of a splendid woodland park, part of which was opened to the public in 1977 to celebrate the Queen's silver jubilee. A maze of paths offers endless opportunities for exploration through gentle wooded valleys and quiet open glades. Returning to the visitor centre, you can then purchase tickets to visit the private gardens and Sandringham House itself.

With your back to the visitor centre and nearby war memorial, head away from the main drive along a gravel path towards the children's play area. Approaching the swings, fork left into the woods to pass between a pair of woodland sculptures **Ⓐ**.

? *Beneath the carved bear holding a spear by the children's play area is a warning, 'Beware the Raven', but where is the raven?*

Carry on through the trees, soon reaching a small clearing. At the far side, bear right onto a narrower path between rhododendron bushes, breaking out past a barrier onto a tarmac drive. Cross to a path opposite and continue forward across grass to a lychgate. A stepped path drops through more shrubbery and another barrier to go by a small bird hide overlooking a secluded pond. Keep on, winding gently downwards along a wooded fold and joining a stream emanating from the pond

PUBLIC TRANSPORT Bus service to visitor centre
REFRESHMENTS Restaurant and tearoom at visitor centre
PUBLIC TOILETS Adjoining visitor centre
PICNIC/PLAY AREA Children's play area close to visitor centre; two picnic sites passed during the first part of the walk
ORDNANCE SURVEY MAPS Explorer 250 (Norfolk Coast West)

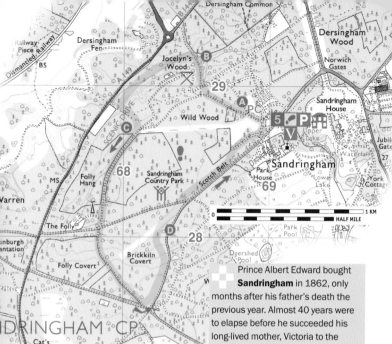

The sculpted bear

Prince Albert Edward bought **Sandringham** in 1862, only months after his father's death the previous year. Almost 40 years were to elapse before he succeeded his long-lived mother, Victoria to the throne, during which time the estate became firmly established as a favourite winter retreat. He demolished much of the original 18th-century house to create a large but comfortable mansion that incorporated splendid state rooms in which to entertain the royal guests. The main rooms are open to the public when the Royal Family are not resident and contain magnificent collections of furniture, porcelain, art and oriental armour.

above. A short distance farther on, watch out for the path swinging away to the left **B**.

Now level, the way runs at the base of a slope, where bracken and

Sandringham House

blackberry brambles spread beneath a shady canopy of oak, birch and pine. Ignoring side paths, keep generally ahead on the main trail, occasional yellow markers confirming your progress. Eventually reaching a prominent junction in front of a larch plantation, go left, climbing onto the edge of a more open heath beside which is a picnic area. Walk through to a tarmac drive and turn right **C**.

Forming part of the estate's Scenic Drive, it runs as an avenue between towering pines before ending through iron gates that were erected in 2002 to mark Queen Elizabeth's golden jubilee. Cross to a gravel track opposite, which curves gently downhill at the edge of Folly Covert. Eventually the track ends at another drive, but immediately before that point, branch left onto a path rising through less wooded ground. Keep going forward past a small reedy pool and then across a clearing. Through more trees at the far side, emerge onto a broad grass ride **D**.

To the right, it ends between a fork as two roads come together. Approaching the junction turn to cross the lane on the left, entering the trees on its far side. The path then swings right to parallel the main drive shortly leading you back to the visitor centre. ●

Holkham

6

START Lady Ann's Drive, Holkham
(grid ref: TF 890446)
DISTANCE 3¼ miles (5.2km)
TIME 1½ hours
PARKING Car park along Lady Ann's Drive (fee)
ROUTE FEATURES Woodland track (initially an easy access route); dune path

The coast at Holkham forms part of the most extensive National Nature Reserve in England, important for the wide range of habitats it contains, which in turn support a great variety of plant and animal species. The walk first follows the edge of a pinewood overlooking grazing reclaimed from the marshes and then returns through the seaward-facing dunes, piled behind an expansive sandy beach. Complete your day with a visit to the hall.

Head along Lady Ann's Drive towards the sea, passing through a white gate at the end into a strip of coastal woodland. Fork left through a second gate and follow a broad track that meanders at the fringe of the trees. After passing Salts Hole, a remnant of a creek that penetrated the marshes to the left, the way leads past the Washington Hide **A**. It is accessible to wheelchairs and offers bird watchers a splendid vantage over the fields where flocks of geese gather to feed. *A wooden walkway continues across the dunes behind to a viewpoint overlooking the coast, and offers a cut-through to point* **C** *for those wishing to shorten the walk.*

> **?** **Why is Salts Hole so named?**

Otherwise, carry on along the track, which soon degrades to grass and passes a couple of cottages. Keep going, ignoring paths on the right into the woods until the way ahead is barred by a gate **B**.

PUBLIC TRANSPORT Bus service along main road
REFRESHMENTS The Victoria and a café at Holkham
PUBLIC TOILETS At Holkham Art, Craft and Fine Food Centre
PICNIC/PLAY AREA Play area for patrons of The Victoria
ORDNANCE SURVEY MAPS Explorer 251 (Norfolk Coast Central)

Swing right, the way narrowing to a winding path that undulates across the wooded ridge to the grass-covered sand dunes.

Emerging from the trees, keep generally ahead as the clear path fragments into the dunes, soon dropping to a distinct crossing path that runs in a shallow trough just beyond and parallel to the trees. To the right it leads back beside the pinewood, eventually passing the viewpoint at the end of the walkway behind the Washington Hide **C**.

The path is a fair way removed from the sea behind a succession of rolling sand dunes, and the easiest route out to the beach lies a little

Covering some 4,000 hectares, the Holkham reserve stretches for almost 15 miles (24km) between Blakeney and Burnham Norton. The **pinewoods** were planted during the late 19th century to help stabilise the dunes and provide shelter from the winds sweeping off the sea. Two types of pine are predominant – Scots and Corsican, the latter being introduced to this country at the end of the 18th century. They can be distinguished by the colour differences of their bark, the Corsican being grey whilst the Scots pine has a reddish-orange hue. Another distinctive tree in the woodland is the **holm oak**, with leaves looking like a cross between oak and holly. Also a Mediterranean species, it thrives in salty coastal winds.

farther along. Past the viewpoint the dunes on the left fall away, eventually enabling the flooding

Holkham beach

rshes

Salts Hole

the beach and climb a path onto the top of the dune. A boarded path takes you back through the woods to the end of Lady Ann's Drive and the car park.

●

The Holkham estate has been held by the Coke family since the beginning of the 17th century. The grand **Palladian mansion** was commissioned by Thomas Coke, the first Earl of Leicester in 1734 as a showcase for art treasures collected during his grand tour. It was his great nephew, also Thomas Coke who was dubbed **'Coke of Norfolk'** and is associated with the great agricultural improvements of the 18th century. Although many of the revolutionary practices were developed by his contemporaries such as 'Turnip Townsend', he introduced new animal breeds to the county and did much to encourage reform and make farming 'fashionable'.

tide to encroach inland. When you reach an area of dune on the right cordoned off by pale fencing, leave

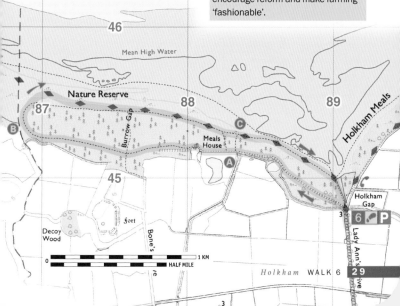

7 *Horsey Windpump*

START Horsey Windpump
(grid ref: TG 456222)
DISTANCE 3¼ miles
(5.2km)
TIME 1¼ hours
PARKING National Trust
car park (Pay and Display,
NT members free)
ROUTE FEATURES Fenland
paths and tracks

Drainage mills were once a common sight across Norfolk's fens and broads but, now replaced by electrical pumps and computer controlled sluices, most are crumbling in decay. The one at Horsey, however, is a spectacular exception, fully restored and a striking landmark amidst a dead flat countryside. The mere and marshes over which it presides attract large numbers of birds, and provide yet another attraction on this undemanding walk.

Leaving the car park beside its entrance, climb onto the raised bank of a broad cut that connects to the mere and follow it right, away from the windpump past boat moorings. Very soon, however, the path veers off beside a boundary ditch. Over to the left, a wooden boathouse hunkered down in the chest-high reeds marks the water's edge, whilst to the right is one of the many copses that provides cover and shelter for wildlife in this otherwise stark landscape. Eventually, the path turns through a gate into a rough field. Strike across to a similar gate opposite and pass back into the fringe of the reed bed **Ⓐ**.

Crossing a ditch, the path continues through reeds and clumps of trees growing along the embankment. Soon the path joins the line of the Waxham New Cut, following it in a near straight line towards another windpump. However, unless the reeds have been recently cut for use as thatching, there is yet little more than an occasional glimpse of it.

Built in 1757, Brograve Drainage Mill is now a ruin; its broken sails

PUBLIC TRANSPORT None
REFRESHMENTS Snack bar at Horsey Windpump and the Nelson Head at Horsey
PUBLIC TOILETS Adjacent to car park
ORDNANCE SURVEY MAPS Explorer OL40 (The Broads)

Throughout the rest of the country, **windmills** were often built on hilltops to catch the wind and were used to grind wheat and other grains, but here in Norfolk, many served a quite different purpose. Like many in Holland, they lifted drainage water from the low-lying land into the banked-up rivers and dikes so that it could flow away to the sea. Replacing an earlier mill, Horsey was erected in 1912 and later superseded by diesel and then finally electricity in 1957.

leaning drunkenly against the weather beaten brick tower, sadly dilapidated and bowed with age. Although its successor, housed in an austere brick box behind might

perform the same function more efficiently, as with much that is 'modern', it contributes nothing to the character of the landscape.

> *Whilst visiting the drainage mill, look at the gear wheels at the base of the central drive shaft. Why do you think that the large crown wheel is toothed in wood, whilst the pinion is of cast iron?*

Once level with the mill **B**, turn away from the cut through the reeds and cross a stile into the sometimes muddy corner of a field. Walk away along the right-hand boundary beside a drain, continuing

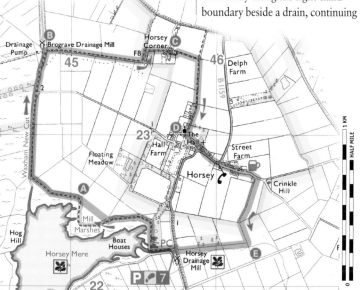

in the subsequent field. At the far side, swing around the corner to a footbridge, cross and stride on towards houses at Horsey Corner C.

Emerging onto a track, go right and then left, winding around the cottages to enter another field. Dog-leg left and right around the corner to follow the margin. At the far side turn right to remain in the field, the way shortly becoming metalled and leading past houses to a junction beside Horsey Church D. A delightful thatched building of flint rubble laid in vague herring-bone patterns, it harks back to the late Saxon era. The original round base of the tower was transformed into an octagonal belfry at the beginning of the 16th century.

Going left, walk through to the main lane and turn left again to pass a flint and brick farmhouse. At a sharp bend by a telephone box, leave the road to carry on along a track facing you. Beyond a large thatched barn and the Nelson Head, look for a permissive path through a field gate on the right a little farther along. *(Note: this path may occasionally be closed in winter for conservation purposes).*

It leads away between open fields, where the distant view is dominated by a wind farm at East Somerton, its hi-tech windmills a sharp contrast to the nostalgia of an earlier age.

Eventually reaching a stile E, where the trees over to the right end to reveal Horsey Windpump once more, cross and turn right. Follow the field edge back to the road, *but be careful crossing for adjacent bushes can obscure a clear view of oncoming traffic.* ●

Horsey Windpump

Walberswick National Nature Reserve

START Walberswick National Nature Reserve, east of Blythburgh (grid ref: TM 470747)
DISTANCE 3½ miles (5.6km)
TIME 1½ hours
PARKING Roadside car park on B1387 at entrance to Walberswick National Nature Reserve
ROUTE FEATURES Woodland paths and tracks

One of several English Nature reserves in the area, Walberswick is the most compact, yet contains within it a great variety of habitats. This short walk takes you through a delightful wood to the reedy marshes bordering the River Blyth, where a hide will detain bird watchers. The pub and church at Blythburgh offer further distractions before returning along an old, hedged track.

Leaving the car park, follow a track into the woods, ignoring a gate on the right. The way falls gently along a heathery swathe that gradually moves away from the road. After ¼ mile (400m) look for a narrow, unmarked trod leaving on the right. It passes between the trees to a path running along a raised bank at the far side **A**, along which you should go left. If you miss it, a second broader path just a little farther on leads to the same place.

Holy Trinity Church at Blythburgh

PUBLIC TRANSPORT None
REFRESHMENTS The White Hart Inn, Blythburgh
PUBLIC TOILETS None
ORDNANCE SURVEY MAPS Explorer 231 (Southwold & Bungay)

Angel Marshes

Hugging the edge of the wood, the way courses above the reeds fringing the marshes. Occasional breaks in the trees allow a view across to the water, whilst ahead is the tall, square tower of Blythburgh Church. Crossing an embankment and stile – *be careful for it can be slippery when wet* – leave the wood behind, in a little while passing a duck-board path into the reeds that leads off to a small hide.

Even from afar, **Blythburgh Church** is impressive, a huge building erected in the 15th century on the profits of the wool trade. Interesting features include **carved pew ends** depicting the seven deadly sins; sloth still in bed and avarice clutching a money chest, whilst the choir stalls did duty as school desks in the Hopton chapel, the pupils' idle graffiti revealing the community's close-knit relationship with the sea. Before you leave, climb a winding staircase to the small **chantry chapel** above the porch; built to accommodate a priest endowed to pray for the Hoptons buried in their chapel.

> **?** *Look amongst the pew end carvings for greed – what is his distinguishing feature?*

Carry on along the main path, shortly passing behind the village pub. Leaving the nature reserve, clamber over a low flood embankment and follow a track out left to the main road **B**. Walk past the White Hart Inn, *crossing with care* to leave just a few paces farther on along Priory Road. Beyond a couple of houses, where once

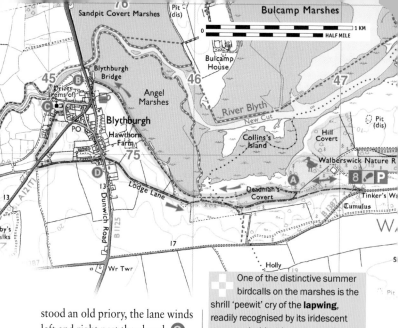

stood an old priory, the lane winds left and right past the church **C**.

Bending left, the way, by now a track, leads past a row of small cottages. At its end, go left into a field and turn right along its edge, leaving at the corner back onto the main road. Cross to the opposite pavement and walk right, but then turn off after 10 yds (9m) onto a track. As it later swings into a paddock, keep ahead on a path, passing behind houses to emerge in the village **D**.

Turn left, but almost immediately, double back right onto a bridleway signed to Walberswick. At first overgrown hedges line the path,

One of the distinctive summer birdcalls on the marshes is the shrill 'peewit' cry of the **lapwing**, readily recognised by its iridescent green and white plumage and the prominent crest curling up from its head. Flocks were once a common sight on ploughed fields across the country, but the use of pesticides has driven them to feed in the more marginal areas where grubs and larvae can still be found. They nest in a simple scrape on the ground, and if you find them flying noisily about as you walk, watch where you are putting your feet.

but later thin to give a final view onto the marshes. Entering the wood, the way runs adjacent to the outward path for a short distance before moving away in favour of slightly higher ground. Continue through the trees, eventually returning to the car park.

9 *Salthouse Marshes*

START Snipes Marsh on A149 between Cley next the Sea and Salthouse (grid ref: TG 060441)
DISTANCE 3½ miles (5.6km)
TIME 1½ hours
PARKING Car park opposite Snipes Marsh
ROUTE FEATURES Field and coastal paths

Left to itself, the tide would lap to the coast road between Cley next the Sea and Salthouse, but it is restrained by a massive shingle bank that claims a ¹/₂-mile (800m) wide strip of pond and marsh that attracts birds in their thousands. This enjoyable walk circles to the east along the low Walsey Hills offering a fine vantage over the marsh, and returns along the coastal defences past a Norfolk Wildlife Trust Nature Reserve.

Cross the road from the car park and follow the verge left past a small pond, Snipes Marsh, turning in just beyond it along a path signed to Salthouse. It leads past the entrance to the Norfolk Ornithological Association Walsey Hills Reserve, a hilltop viewpoint that looks out across the marshes. The route, however, continues ahead through an almost tunnel-like thicket of blackthorn before breaking out at the edge of an open field Ⓐ.

Go left beside the hedge for some

Cley Marshes was the country's first Wildlife Trust reserve, established in 1926 by Dr Sydney Long to ensure its protection for the benefit of the countless birds who breed or pass through each year. It is one of the few places in Britain where **bittern** regularly breed, a secretive bird that is related to the heron. The bittern builds its nest deep in the reed beds and the bird's presence is more often revealed by its call, a deep resonant booming that can travel for more than one mile (1.6km) in still air.

15 yds (14m) to an internal corner, and then bear right, striking up the field on a cleared path through the

PUBLIC TRANSPORT Bus service along main road
REFRESHMENTS The Dun Cow in Salthouse
PUBLIC TOILETS By the Dun Cow in Salthouse
ORDNANCE SURVEY MAPS Explorer 251 (Norfolk Coast Central)

crop. Over the crest, a panorama opens across the marshes to the distant embankment, the often bird-crowded ponds of Arnold's Marsh and Cley Marshes lying before it. Passing through a gap at the far side of the field, continue in the same direction making for the crenellated tower of Salthouse Church that now becomes visible on the skyline. Over a crossing track bear left, heading towards the ruin of a wartime pillbox below the scrub of Sarbury Hill **B**.

Climb to the top of the slope and continue at the field edge. After dropping through the subsequent meadow, follow a contained path between gardens to come out in the village beside The Green **C**.

The Dun Cow lies just to the left facing a triangular village green, whilst the walk continues to the right along Purdy Street. After 130 yds (119m), just past a street onto a small residential estate, turn off left into a narrow passage between flint barns. The path leads to the churchyard at the top of the hill.

? *What is a 'Dun Cow'?*

Amongst the treasures inside St Nicholas's are pieces of a 16th-century rood screen, whose painted wooden panels depict apostles and kings. Walk around the church to leave at its eastern end, dropping out at the bottom onto a village

Cley Windmill

in profusion. The fleshy stems of glasswort help it retain water in the salty conditions in which it thrives. Its name derives from the fact that it was used to make glass; the ash of the plant when burned has a high potash content, an essential ingredient for the process. Climb onto the shingle bank behind, and head to the left. The distant village is Cley next the Sea, its attractive cottages dominated by an 18th-century windmill that is open to visitors during the summer. The village church, lying just a little way inland, is also worth visiting.

lane. Go left and walk along to the main road **D**.

Turn left again, passing some cottages. At the end of the row, cross to a track opposite that strikes out over the marsh. After crossing a drain in the middle, continue towards a prominent sandy hill dubbed 'Little Eye'. During the Second World War, its elevated position was exploited as an observation post and gun position.

Dog-leg to avoid a small pool at its foot, around which sea aster and glasswort are to be found growing

Keep going for just over one mile (1.6km) until, after passing two large ponds on Arnold's Marsh and drawing level with the end of the Walsey Hills, you will see a track below you running inland **E**. Following the eastern boundary of the Cley Marshes Nature Reserve, it returns you to the car park. To visit the reserve, you must first buy a ticket from the visitor centre, which lies a little farther along the road towards Cley next the Sea. ●

The North Walsham and Dilham Canal

START East Ruston (grid ref: TG 346272)
DISTANCE 3½ miles (5.6km)
TIME 1½ hours
PARKING Weavers' Way car park, East Ruston
ROUTE FEATURES Tracks and field paths

10

Although incalculable miles of drains, cuts and river channels have been dug in Norfolk over the centuries, strangely, it has only one true canal, the North Walsham and Dilham. This delightful walk combines a picturesque stretch with part of the Weavers' Way, which here follows the line of a disused railway.

Leave the back of the car park onto the Weavers' Way and follow it right a little distance to pass through a gate beside a cottage. Turning sharp left, walk along a track, which shortly passes a couple of houses to end at a gate. Carry on ahead beside a hedge at the edge of rough fenland grazing, later crossing a stile to continue in the next field.

Passing through a gate opening at the far side **A**, strike out on a right diagonal to the distant corner to meet the canal. Go over a stile on the left and walk beside the waterway to Tonnage Bridge **B**. It gives a fine vantage over the canal, although you have to be very tall to see over the high walls.

? **What do the fruits of the alder tree look like?**

Cross the bridge, but instead of following the ongoing track away, leave it almost immediately into the field on the right to regain the canal bank. A path skirts the field beside the water. Beyond a couple of cultivated fields, the path

PUBLIC TRANSPORT None
REFRESHMENTS None
PUBLIC TOILETS None
ORDNANCE SURVEY MAPS Explorer 252 (Norfolk Coast East) or Explorer OL40 (The Broads)

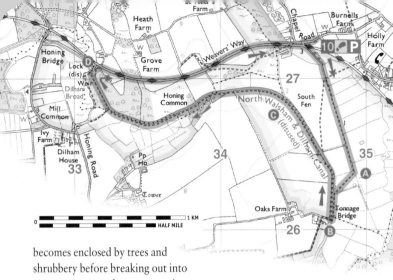

becomes enclosed by trees and shrubbery before breaking out into more open ground once more. A little farther on the canal swings past a junction, where a cut draining fens around East Ruston enters **C**.

Beyond there, the way passes into a wetland copse. The wood is dominated by alder; one of the first trees to become established in Britain from warmer continental Europe as the glaciers retreated northwards at the end of the last Ice Age. Emerging into grazing at the other side, the route continues by the canal at the edge of a succession of lush meadows. As you cross a stream into the last meadow, at the far side of which is more woodland, notice that its waters are augmented by an underground spring that bubbles up from between the stones on its bed.

Approaching the wood, the field edge curves away from the canal beside a ditch. Look for a plank bridge that takes the way through the reeds to a gate and walk on into the wood, the path then swinging right to regain the canal. Twisting between the trees, you shortly reach a clearing beside Honing Lock **D**.

Be careful above the crumbling brick walls lining the lock, as the cut is quite deep. Still evident, despite its ruinous condition, are the sluices through which the lock was filled and emptied, as too are the supports on which the heavy gates once swung. The canal is fed by the River Ant, and its waters flow over the upper sill to create one of the very few, if not the only 'waterfall' you are likely to see in the whole of Norfolk.

A footbridge at the far end of the lock takes the path into a copse on the other bank, emerging beyond it onto a drive. Go left and then immediately right to join the Weavers' Way through a gate. It is about one mile's walk (1.6km) back to the car park, but there is much of interest along the way. Young trees form the hedges on either side, at the base of which a succession of wild flowers appear through the seasons. Keep a look out for the occasional sweet-smelling honeysuckle, and as summer draws to a close, there is no shortage of blackberries. Eventually, the track passes through

The **North Walsham and Dilham Canal** was dogged from the very start. Opposition from established businesses delayed its construction for 13 years until it was finally opened in 1826. Built to accommodate small wherries transporting agricultural produce and coal, it ran for nine miles (14.5km) between Antingham Ponds and Weyford Bridge. By 1893 however the top section had been abandoned, with more being closed after flooding in 1912. The last cargo left Bacton Wood in 1934, after which the waterway quickly became derelict.

more boggy woodland surrounding the outflow of Hundred Stream, then passes a fishing pool before reaching a crossing track. The car park from which you began is just a few paces farther along the Weavers' Way on the left.

Honing Lock

11 Burnham Deepdale and Brancaster Marsh

START St Mary's Church, Burnham Deepdale (grid ref: TF 804443)

DISTANCE $4\frac{1}{4}$ miles (6.8km)

TIME $1\frac{3}{4}$ hours

PARKING Street parking near church at Burnham Deepdale

ROUTE FEATURES Coast and field paths

When the Romans arrived in Britain, Brancaster lay at the edge of the land, and it was above the shore that they built a substantial fort. In the centuries that have passed since then, accumulating sand has pushed the sea away, and over one mile (1.6km) of intervening saltings and dunes now separate it from the open water. Leading to the fort over low inland hills, the walk wanders back along the coast to reveal yet more aspects of Norfolk's character.

From the church, which contains a remarkable 12th-century font, walk along the main road past a garage, crossing to take the first turning off on the left, Delgate Lane. Beyond the last of the houses, you can enter the fields on the right and follow a parallel path at the margin. Approaching Valley Farm, return to the lane and continue climbing alongside a wood. Passing a stand of impressive beech trees at the top of the hill, the lane swings right to fall beside an open field.

? *How many lions are carved upon the font in Burnham Deepdale's church?*

Reaching a junction at the bottom **A** go right, but then leave immediately onto a waymarked path. It rises along a shallow valley at the edge of a wood, curving away higher up to continue beside Barrow Common. As you broach the crest **B**, there is a view to the coast ahead.

PUBLIC TRANSPORT Bus service to Burnham Deepdale

REFRESHMENTS Lazy Lounge Café and the White Horse in Burnham Deepdale; seafood snack bar at Brancaster Staithe

PUBLIC TOILETS None

ORDNANCE SURVEY MAPS Explorer 250 (Norfolk Coast West)

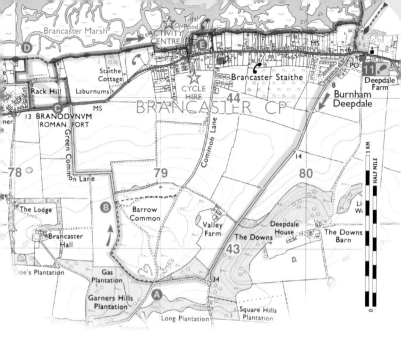

Carry on at the perimeter of the common as a path joins from the right, leaving through a gate at the corner. A broad grassy drove, Green Common Lane, leads the way down the far side of the hill. Meeting a crossing track part way down go left, and then at the next junction right and walk on to reach the main road at the bottom **C**.

Cross to a narrow gap opposite, through which a kissing-gate leads into the corner of an open grass field. It was here that Branodunum Roman Fort once stood, enclosing a large square over to the left. Nothing remains above ground of

the high defensive wall or the buildings that stood within it, yet the surviving outer ditch is still an impressive feature and hints at the

Although parts of its walls were still standing to a height of over 12ft (3m) in the 17th century, much of the history of **Brancaster's Roman fort** is obscure. Built during the 3rd century and occupied by a cavalry regiment, Branodunum was part of a sporadic line of coastal defences set against Saxon raiders. It remained garrisoned for some 200 years, during which time a busy civilian settlement developed around it. After the Romans left the place appears to have remained in use and was re-fortified by the Normans.

The saltings below Burnham Deepdale

dominance the fort would have exerted over the area in its day.

Strike a diagonal through the centre of the fort, leaving the field by a gate in the distant corner. Cross a track to a second gate opposite and head directly across to yet another gate at the far side, exiting through that onto the coast path **D**.

Turn right at the edge of the salt marsh. Stretching away is a vast expanse of shimmering feathery reeds that sing in the wind. Around the fringe, clumps of greater willow herb add streaks of pink and, in the skies above, you might spot curlews patrolling the distant mud flats and creeks. Eventually reaching Brancaster Staithe, the path ends

through a gate. Go forward past a row of attractive gabled cottages overlooking a small green to a junction and turn left to the beach at Brancaster Sailing Club **E**.

The coast path continues on the right through the boat park, signed to Burnham Overy Staithe. Carry on above muddy creeks to a crossing track. Go left and immediately right to pass between a brick-built store and a corrugated shed. The way continues above the tide line on top of a low bank, raised to protect the long gardens that run down to the sea from former fishermen's cottages. Meeting a crossing track at the end of the houses, turn right and follow it away from the coast to return to Burnham Deepdale. ●

Dingle Marshes

Dunwich is a place to excite the imagination, as most of this once thriving trading port has been swept away by the waves and the last two millennia have seen the coast move inland over 1¼ miles (2km). The walk traces the fringe of Dunwich Forest before returning along the shingle bank, which, for the time being at least, holds the encroaching sea at bay.

START Dunwich (grid ref: TM 479707)
DISTANCE 4¼ miles (6.8km)
TIME 1¾ hours
PARKING Beach car park (voluntary donations)
ROUTE FEATURES Woodland track; shingle bank

Leaving the car park, follow the lane back and turn right to go through the village, passing first The Ship and then the village museum. Carry on until you reach a junction by St James's Church and there go right again. Just after crossing a bridge spanning Dunwich River, abandon the lane for a track on the right Ⓐ.

Ignoring the entrances to the Bridge Nurseries and the Phoenix Centre in the old thatched barn, carry on along a gently rising hedged track between the fields beyond. Reaching the edge of the forest, it

Although now barely a hamlet, **Dunwich** was once one of the most important trading ports in the whole of East Anglia. Its entry in the Domesday survey records 3,000 inhabitants and 80 sizeable ships at a time when most places were little more than a collection of hovels. Disaster struck in 1286, when storms shifted the line of the coast cutting off the harbour. Ever since, the low cliffs have been crumbling into the sea, the last of the town's original nine churches finally disappearing in 1918. You can find out more about the medieval town in the **small museum**.

continues at the fringe of the woodland. Keep an eye open for squirrels as there are plenty about,

PUBLIC TRANSPORT None
REFRESHMENTS Café overlooking car park; tearoom at Bridge Nurseries and The Ship in Dunwich village
PUBLIC TOILETS Beside car park
ORDNANCE SURVEY MAPS Explorer 231 (Southwold & Bungay)

Point Marsh

Dingle Great
Hill

73

B Great Dingle
Farm

Sandymount
Covert

Foxburrow
Wood

Dingle Stone
House

8

72

Dingle Marshes

Reedland Marshes

wich
est

Little Dingle

48

71

Bridge
Farm

A 2

IMI

P

PC

12 **P**

Maison Dieu Hill

Chapel
(rems of)
Dunwich

8

Remains of
Friary
(Franciscan)

C

Mean High Wat

Mean Low Water

1 KM

HALF MILE

0

Horned poppy

and breaks in the trees allow views
across the reedy expanse of Dingle
Marshes. Carry on, in due course
passing in turn Little Dingle, some
cottages and Dingle Stone House.
The track then curves around,
eventually breaking from the forest
through a gate.

Go forward through gorse and
scrub to a clearing, there joining
another track **B**, which to the
right leads past Great Dingle Farm.

? *What two objects are
displayed outside the
museum?*

Dunwich friary

Keep going through a gate, the path riding an embankment across the marsh towards a low bracken-covered hill. Swinging around its landward side, the path leads to a junction overlooking a broad ditch, Dunwich River **C**.

Follow the path to the right, now winding towards the shingle bank, splashed throughout the summer with the bright yellow flowers of horned poppies. Climb onto the top and turn right back towards Dunwich. The loose pebbles do not make for fast walking, but once past the lagoons you can drop to an easier path below on the landward side of the ridge. *In spring and summer, watch where you put your feet and respect any areas that are fenced off to protect the nests and young of little tern and ringed plover.* Another mile's walking (1.6km) brings you back to the beach car park. ●

A ruined stone building set behind a high, gated wall on the edge of the village is all that remains of a medieval **Franciscan friary**. Called 'Grey Friars' from the colour of their habit, the mendicants followed a life of poverty and chastity, wandering among the scattered villages preaching and offering what practical help they could to the poor and the sick. The friars were evicted at the Dissolution between 1536 and 1539 and the buildings were plundered for their stone. What remained was subsequently occupied as a house and then served as the town hall and prison until finally being abandoned at the beginning of the 19th century.

13 *Thurne*

START Thurne
(grid ref: TG 403158)
DISTANCE 4½ miles
(7.2km)
TIME 1¾ hours
PARKING Roadside
parking in village
ROUTE FEATURES Riverside
and field paths

Life on the Broads revolves around the water and the rivers have long been the best ways of getting around. The River Thurne feeds the River Yare by way of the River Bure and must be one of the strangest rivers going. Its source lies barely a stone's throw from the coast, yet the waters meander for some 28 miles (45km) before being loosed to the sea at Yarmouth. This gentle walk follows the river between Thurne and Repps, returning cross country, through a wood and past a thatched church with an unusual squint.

39

Leave the centre of the village almost opposite The Lion Inn, following a path beside the moorings with the water on your left towards a drainage mill. Reaching the River Thurne, turn right to pass around the mill and follow a path, not quite at the water's edge – it is distanced from it by a thick belt of reeds.

Who rescued Thurne Dyke Drainage Mill from dereliction?

Overlooking the banks of the river from which it takes its name, Thurne stands on the landward side of a low, irregularly shaped island that separates the fens from the sea. The river is tidal for almost its entire length and, left to its own devices, the marshes would be flooded with brackish waters. The two mills by the village staithe were built during the 19th century to lift water from the drainage ditches surrounding the fields into the river so that it could flow away with the falling tide. **Thurne Dyke Drainage Mill**, passed as you turn onto the riverbank, is occasionally operated. For details contact the **Norfolk Windmills Trust.**

PUBLIC TRANSPORT None
REFRESHMENTS The Lion Inn, Thurne
PUBLIC TOILETS Opposite start of walk in village
PICNIC/PLAY AREA Picnic site on the riverside at Repps
ORDNANCE SURVEY MAPS Explorer OL40 (The Broads)

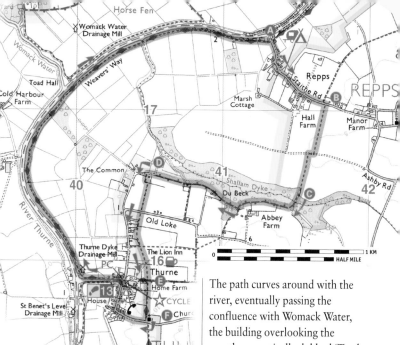

The summer busyness of traffic passing along the river is not a modern phenomenon, for the twisting channels penetrate the heart of productive farmland and boat was by far the easiest way to move produce to markets and coastal ports for export. A specialised boat called a 'wherry' was developed to do the job. Shallow drafted to navigate the higher reaches, the vessel's mast and sail can be readily lowered to enable it to slip beneath the low-arched bridges that span the streams.

The path curves around with the river, eventually passing the confluence with Womack Water, the building overlooking the mouth romantically dubbed 'Toad Hall'. Beyond there, set back in the fields is the ruin of another drainage mill. Farther on, a straggle of moorings and waterside chalets deprive you of a river view and herald your approach to Repps. At the end of the huts the bank is given over to a pleasant picnic area where, for the first time since leaving Thurne, you can actually get to the water's edge Ⓐ.

Reaching a tarmac lane just beyond, follow it away from the river, winding past cottages and houses and then Hall Farm. Carry on a little farther, to reach a track on the left beside a bungalow, Dewbeck View . It serves to mark the point at which you leave the lane, turning into the large field on the right. Walk directly away across the middle towards a signpost visible at the far side. Cross a grass track and continue on the same heading to a wood beyond. Walk ahead past an injutting corner to the far boundary, where a footbridge takes the path across a dike into the trees .

Press through to the far side and, ignoring a footbridge in front, turn right onto a path that remains in the wood, skirting its southern perimeter. Shortly reaching a waymarked crossing of paths, go right to continue on a bridleway at the edge of the trees. Grassy swathes take the track past two successive cottages before it eventually passes a third house .

Immediately past the building, turn off the track at a waymark to follow a contained path that by-passes its garden. Walk away over the field behind. Reaching a narrow lane at the far side, cross to the field opposite and continue in the same direction across successive enclosures until you emerge onto a track at Home Farm .

Go left past the farm-house to a stile on the right, climbing that to resume your southerly direction across the fields, now making for Thurne Church . Walk out to the lane and follow it to the right, shortly ending up back in the village from which you began the walk. ●

Thurne Dyke Drainage Mill

Roydon Common

Despite its seemingly wild appearance, Roydon Common is a carefully managed landscape, maintained as open ground to preserve the unique balance of plant and animal life that developed over the centuries when it was used as common grazing. Around it in contrast are the large fields created by present day farming practice and extensive tracts of woodland.

START Roydon Common Nature Reserve, west of Roydon
(grid ref: TF 679228)
DISTANCE 3¾ miles (7.6km)
TIME 2 hours
PARKING Car park off minor lane, ¾ mile (1.2km) east of junction between A148 and A149
ROUTE FEATURES Woodland; heath and field paths and tracks

14

Walk back to the lane from the car park, cross and go left. After 200 yds (183m), turn off through a broad gap in the hedge on the right (ignore the stile immediately before it) and head away from the road with the field boundary on your right. After 50 yds (46m), turn right again over a stile and climb the edge of a long field beside a sparse hedge. Joining a field track at the top corner, dog-leg through an opening to maintain your direction in the adjacent field, re-crossing the hedge beyond the crest. Eventually passing some large barns, the track leads into Hall Farm. Meeting a concrete track at the end, follow it left up to meet the lane **A**.

Walk to the right as far as the next bend, but then abandon the lane in favour of a bridleway that continues straight ahead. Becoming a leafy tunnel it leads to a crossing of tracks by cottages. Go left but immediately leave through a gate on the right onto a small common where you might find Exmoor ponies. Strike across to a fence at the far side and turn right on a path beside it, passing through birch wood and eventually emerging over a stile onto a lane **B**.

PUBLIC TRANSPORT None
REFRESHMENTS Blacksmith's Arms in nearby Roydon
PUBLIC TOILETS None
ORDNANCE SURVEY MAPS Explorer 250 (Norfolk Coast West)

Cross to a grassy track opposite, the bed of a disused railway, and follow it through a gate, looking for a small gate some 200 yds (183m) along on the left. Go through that and head directly away towards a belt of trees, turning left when you reach them to follow the perimeter fence. The path leads out to a lane **C**.

Turn right and walk as far as a junction with Chequers Road, there leaving through a kissing-gate on the right. A long straight path leads away beside a deep drainage ditch at the edge of Hudson's Fen. It later bends left to parallel the course of the old railway encountered earlier, ultimately ending through a kissing-gate by houses **D**.

Turn right onto a rough track. Breaking out from the trees, it continues at the edge of a vast expanse of open heath. Follow it

for a good ½ mile (800m), until you eventually reach a gate on the right through which is signed a footpath **E**. It winds out across the heath, gently curving around the base of a prominent sandy hillock and keeping above the boggy ground that falls away to the right. Finally meeting a crossing track, go right, soon passing through a gate to return to the parking area. ●

One of the prettiest and most distinctive plants growing on the heath is the **bog asphodel**, and between July and September it forms clumps of golden flowers that turn to orange as the seeds form. In some places it is known as **maiden hair**, because its flowers were collected and infused to create a yellow wash used by girls to colour their hair.

The vast heath of Roydon Common

Exmoor ponies on Roydon Common

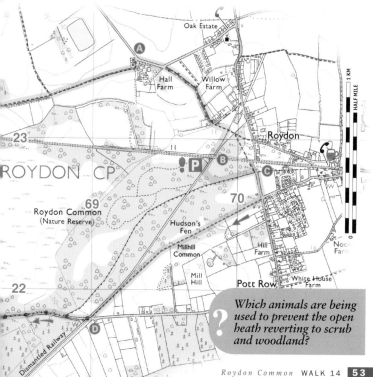

Which animals are being used to prevent the open heath reverting to scrub and woodland?

15 Snettisham Coastal Park

START Snettisham Scalp, west of Snettisham (grid ref: TF 648335)

DISTANCE 5 miles (8km)

TIME 2 hours

PARKING Beach car park (fee)

ROUTE FEATURES Dune and dike paths

A large proportion of the Norfolk coast is protected within nature reserves, each subtly different from its neighbour. Here parallel embankments overlook very distinct habitats, the low-tide banks of the Wash drawing waders, reed beds and reclaimed grazing attracting winter flocks of pink-footed geese, and between them a wetland, the former course of the River Heacham. The walk takes in both banks and has something to offer at any time of the year.

Leaving the car park the walk begins along the coastal strip, heading to the right either along the top of the broad shingle and earth embankment or, if the tide is right, on the beach below. Beyond the reach of the waves, the bank is well colonised by hardy plants such as sea rocket and the distinctive yellow horned poppy. Farther back from the water dense thickets of sea buckthorn grow, easily recognised by its striking orange berry.

One of the most conspicuous plants along the shingle is the **yellow horned poppy**. It was once valued for its medicinal properties and according to Culpeper, the 17th-century herbalist, could be taken to open obstructions of the liver and spleen as well as acting as an antidote to plague. Applied to the skin it would cure ringworm, scurvy and 'tetters' – whatever that might have been. However, should you suffer any of these ailments, you would be better advised to visit your doctor, as the plant is quite poisonous and affects the brain.

PUBLIC TRANSPORT None

REFRESHMENTS Café behind the beach at Heacham serving ice cream, snacks and hot food

PUBLIC TOILETS Behind the beach at Heacham

PICNIC/PLAY AREA Picnic site behind the car park at Snettisham Scalp

ORDNANCE SURVEY MAPS Explorer 250 (Norfolk Coast West)

A little way along, the sea defences are consolidated within a broad wall, on top of which a small hide overlooks the expansive flats of the Wash exposed by the ebbing tides. These are rich feeding grounds and well frequented by many species of waders, probing the mud and sand with their long beaks for food. Standing back, almost one mile (1.6km) inland, a wooded scarp rises, the coastline of an earlier age. Farther on, beyond the end of the wall, the bank reverts to shingle and then dune, bound together with coarse marram grass.

In a little while a large pool appears below to the right, a path sloping down the embankment to its foot. *You can, if you wish, shorten the walk at this point* **A**,

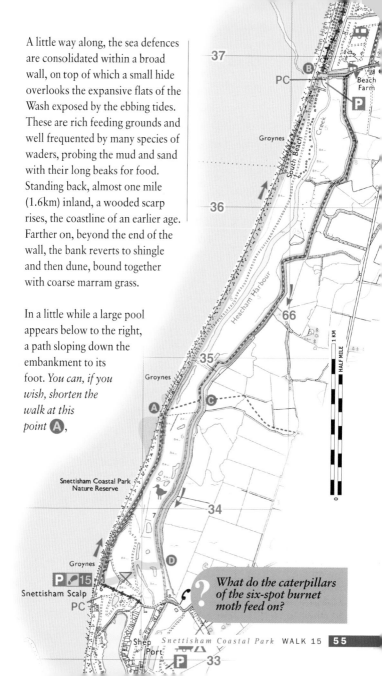

What do the caterpillars of the six-spot burnet moth feed on?

Snettisham Coastal Park WALK 15 **55**

by crossing the depression to a second inland bank **C**, *where you will pick up the return path to the car park.* Otherwise carry on along the sand dunes towards Heacham. At South Beach, a line of chalets shelters behind the dunes, a development sparked by the post-war growth in prosperity and car ownership. The modern-day equivalent, the static caravan, herds separately a little farther on.

After passing a sluice that controls the present outlet of Heacham River, leave the beach and follow a road inland to the entrance of a car park, where you will find a café and toilets **B**. Crossing the river, carry on for another 150 yds (137m) to find a waymarked footpath climbing right onto the

Along the shore at Snettisham

embankment above the road. Over a stile on the right, follow it away, passing a couple of wartime bunkers lying in the rough field below you.

Although hardly distant from the coastal ridge, the vegetation here is completely different from that encountered during the first part of the walk, the grassy bank supporting an abundance of thistle, ragwort, bramble, dog rose and a veritable forest of teasel. Walk on for a little over 1½ miles (2.4km), with the old river course on your right, now a reedy creek and known as Heacham Harbour. Below to the left, a long ditch drains the reclaimed pastures won from the marshes. The way eventually crosses a stile **C**, where the shortcut path joins from the right. Keep walking for another ¾ mile (1.2km) to draw level with the car park. Look for a post marking a stepped path down the right-hand side of the embankment **D**, and follow that across the nature reserve wetland. Meeting a broader path towards the far side, follow it briefly left before forking right to return past the picnic area to the car park. ●

Mannington Hall

START Mannington Hall (grid ref: TG 140321)
DISTANCE 5 miles (8km)
TIME 2¼ hours
PARKING Car park at Mannington Hall (fee-paying, but free to garden visitors)
ROUTE FEATURES Field tracks and woodland paths

Set amidst Norfolk's gentle rolling countryside and renowned for its rose and ornamental flower gardens, Mannington Hall makes a great place for a day out. Miles of footpaths and permissive ways explore the estate woodlands and carrs, which are managed for the diversity of wildlife that they attract and offer many opportunities for interesting walks, short or long.

Turning right out of the visitor centre car park, follow the lane away from the main gates, avoiding the tarmac by a parallel path running through the trees on the left. After ¼ mile (400m), look for a gravel farm track leading left through a gate (A). Beyond a rambling byre, it rises between the fields, later passing a second barn before descending to a junction at the corner of Mossymere Wood. Wind forward with the ongoing track, which curves around the eastern edge of the wood. When you reach a sharp right-hand bend,

Mannington Hall

keep ahead on an ancient hedged way, and over a stile at the end

PUBLIC TRANSPORT None
REFRESHMENTS Tearoom at Mannington Hall (in season) and the Walpole Arms at Itteringham
PUBLIC TOILETS For visitors to Mannington Gardens
PICNIC/PLAY AREA For visitors to Mannington Gardens
ORDNANCE SURVEY MAPS Explorer 252 (Norfolk Coast East)

walk on through thicket to find a crossing path .

> Dating from the middle of the 15th century, **Mannington Hall** is one of the most picturesque buildings in the area with richly ornamented chimneys rising above embattled walls and turrets, which are pierced by rows of mullioned windows that gaze across a shimmering moat. Bought by Horatio Walpole, younger brother to Britain's first Prime Minister, during the early part of the 18th century, it is a complete contrast to the crisp Georgian architecture of the mansion he was then building in nearby Wolterton Park. Mannington's gardens, created by the present Lord Walpole, are open during the season, as is the hall at Wolterton.

Turn right beside the gorse and bramble fringe of a wetland wood, shortly emerging onto a track, which leads left over a stream into the village. Whilst The Walpole Arms lies a little distance to the right, the onward way is left along the lane past St Mary's Church. Opposite cottages at the crest of the hill and immediately after passing a track leaving the lane, enter the field on the left and accompany the hedge away. Penetrating trees at the bottom, keep forward over a plank bridge spanning a ditch . To the right, a path winds through the coppice, later swinging right over a stile into the corner of a meadow. Strike out to join the opposite boundary and follow it left beside a wood, eventually meeting a lane .

If you wish to shorten the walk, the car park lies only ¼ mile (400m) to the left, however, there is still much to see. Cross to a gate opposite and continue at the edge of another meadow, where there is a fine view across the moat and lakes to Mannington Hall. Keep going until you reach a gate by Hall Farm, turning left just before it to follow the boundary fence down to a second gate. Carry on along a grass track, passing through another gate at its end to cross the bottom edge

Beside the stream at Itteringham

of a rough meadow. Over a stile to the left of a gate near the corner, keep ahead on a path bordering a woodland strip. At the end, climb into the field on the right and cut a diagonal to a stile in its far corner. Carry on along the right-hand side of a long, rough pasture, the square tower of St Andrew's Church soon coming into view ahead. Through a gate at the top corner, a field track leads left past a cottage to emerge in Little Barningham **E**.

Follow the lane left through the village, turning left again towards Saxthorpe when you reach a crossroads. After ⅓ mile (540m), where the road curves in a pronounced right-hand bend, leave beside a waypost on the left into the adjacent field. Cut across the bottom corner and turn left along the perimeter. Passing through a gap at the top into the next field, immediately turn right on a peripheral track. After twisting around the intrusive corner of a small pinewood, Oak Grove, go left to remain in the same field, following the track out to a lane. The car park is then only a short walk to the left. ●

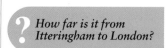

? *How far is it from Itteringham to London?*

17 *Dunwich Heath and Minsmere Marsh*

START Dunwich Heath (grid ref: TM 476677)
DISTANCE 5 miles (8km)
TIME 2 hours
PARKING National Trust car park (Pay and Display, NT members free)
ROUTE FEATURES Heathland; field tracks and paths

Although sitting side by side on the Suffolk coast, Dunwich Heath and Minsmere Marsh are two very different nature reserves. The first is a sandy heath of grass, heather and woodland, whilst the mere is a watery expanse of reedy pools. The walk takes you by both, returning along the coast where there is a public hide overlooking the RSPB reserve.

Beginning from the entrance to the car park beside the former coastguard cottages, follow a path inland past Heath Barn and a small picnic area onto the heathery heath. Over a rise, the path gently undulates downwards, entering rich woodland of oak, birch, sweet chestnut and Scots pine.

Ignoring side paths, keep generally ahead on the main track until you

? *By the picnic area at the start of the walk is an upright wooden board – what creature is carved upon it?*

eventually reach a T-junction. Go along it to the left, shortly breaking out from the trees onto a metalled lane **A**, which to the left leads to the RSPB Minsmere Reserve's Visitor Centre. The route, however,

PUBLIC TRANSPORT None
REFRESHMENTS Coastguard tearoom next to car park; Eels Foot Inn at Eastbridge
PUBLIC TOILETS By the car park
PICNIC/PLAY AREA Small play area near former coastguard cottages; picnic site by Heath Barn
ORDNANCE SURVEY MAPS Explorer 212 (Woodbridge & Saxmundham) and Explorer 231 (Southwold & Bungay)

The view across Dunwich Heath

lies ahead, crossing to the track directly opposite. It passes through grazing, where you should keep you eyes open, as there are often small groups of red deer to be seen, feeding on the grass. Over to the left, is a view across the Minsmere marshes to the coast, where a little farther to the south a white dome and concrete block house the twin Sizewell nuclear power stations.

Cresting Saunders' Hill the track delves into the gruesomely named Hangman's New Wood and then meets the corner of a lane **B**. It too leads left into the RSPB reserve, but you should instead follow it ahead, before long

The **heathland** at Dunwich is one of Britain's rarest habitats and entirely man-made. After the clearing of the original wild wood at the end of the Stone Age, the land gradually became acid rich and nutrient poor, with sheep later being turned onto the sparse grassland to graze. Left untended, birch, bramble and bracken would quickly smother the bedstraw, heather and gorse, destroying the fragile environment that supports adders, grass snakes, slow worms and common lizards as well as a wide range of insects and spiders.

reaching a sharp bend where a sandy track joins from the right **C**. Swing left with the lane to cross Minsmere River and the head of the marsh. Soon entering

Eastbridge, keep left at a fork to pass the Eels Foot Inn, which makes a convenient stopping place for lunch **D**.

Low cliffs fringe the sand and shingle shore

A short distance beyond the pub, and immediately after passing the last of the roadside cottages on the left (which, incidentally has a Victorian letterbox built into its wall) turn off left on a track, signed to Minsmere Sluice. Then, just beyond another cottage, look for a contained path leaving on the right, which winds around the edge of a field before turning east towards

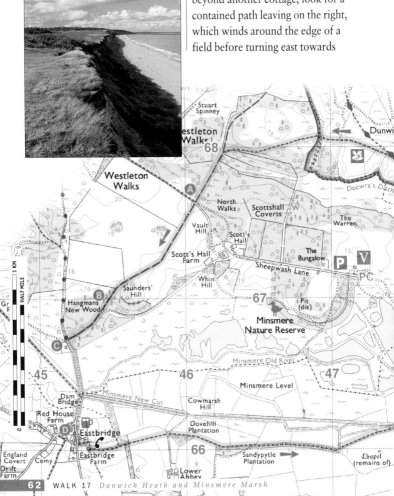

the coast. Carry on as it later strikes out between fields, passing through a gate at the far side.

A track leads left to a second gate, through which, turn right along a grass track that runs beside a drainage ditch. Carry on over a stile, eventually reaching another gate. Again go left and then right, following a strip of rough meadow beside a large field to your right. In the middle stands the lonely ruin of an old chapel. Its history is somewhat obscure, but it is believed to have been a dependant of the Premonstratensian abbey that was a little way to the south towards Leiston. Now roofless, its rough-coursed walls of pebble are crumbling, but enough remained during the last war to camouflage a gun emplacement, placed inside at its eastern end where the altar would once have stood.

The coast lies just a little farther on, the path climbing above a sluice gate that controls the outflow of Minsmere River to the sea **E**. Paths run left back to the coastguard cottages at Dunwich Heath, both on top of the shingle bank (which although offering a splendid view across the pools of the RSPB reserve can be hard going because of the loose pebbles underfoot) or below, beside the perimeter fence. Alternatively, at low tide, you have the option of walking along the beach at the edge of the water.

Not far along there is a public hide overlooking the marsh, a good place to take out your binoculars and watch the birds on the water. In summer, keep a look out for the avocet, easily distinguished by its black and white markings and long upturned bill. A little farther on, there is a second hide, but this is located just inside the reserve and is only open to RSPB members or those who have purchased a ticket from the visitor centre.

If you've followed the beach or the top of the shingle bank, as you approach Minsmere Cliffs, you must cross to the path on the landward side of the embankment. It winds around the base of a sandy bluff to return you to the car park.

18 *Thorpeness*

START	Sizewell (grid ref: TM 474628)
DISTANCE	5¼ miles (8.4km)
TIME	2¼ hours
PARKING	Beach car park (Pay and Display)
ROUTE FEATURES	Dune paths; heath tracks

Thorpeness achieved a modicum of fame at the beginning of the 20th century when it was chosen by Glencairn Stuart Ogilvy for the site of a purpose-built holiday village. With mock Tudor buildings, prim gardens and a boating lake it was a place where affluent Edwardians brought their families and servants to relax by the sea. Following an enjoyable coastal stroll from neighbouring Sizewell, the walk returns from Thorpeness across a delightful heathy common where plant and wildlife flourish within a local conservation area.

From the car park, walk back along the road to the corner and turn off left onto a track. Where that then bends towards a row of timber-clad houses, keep ahead below them past a barrier and a scattering of fishermen's shacks. A path runs on through the dunes, going by a row of beach huts to pick a way through the prickly gorse, bramble, bracken and marram grass beyond.

Keeping at the landward side of the dunes, where the going is generally easier than on the soft sand or shingle, the way skirts a small caravan site Ⓐ into a fringe of stunted sycamore. The path then delves into a curious tunnel, taking it under a private garden terrace overlooking the beach below Sizewell House. Thickets of holm oak line the onward way, which continues past wartime defences at the perimeter of the garden walls of two more large houses.

Private land now extends to the edge of the dunes and you are

PUBLIC TRANSPORT Bus service to Thorpeness
REFRESHMENTS Beach café (Sizewell 'T') and Vulcan Arms at Sizewell; choice of cafés and pub at Thorpeness
PUBLIC TOILETS At both Sizewell and Thorpeness
PICNIC/PLAY AREA Boats for hire on The Meare at Thorpeness
ORDNANCE SURVEY MAPS Explorer 212 (Woodbridge & Saxmundham)

forced to pursue a lower line by the shingle. The coast soon gently curves to bring Thorpeness into view ahead and before long, houses appear above, perched on top of the sandy slopes clamouring for the best view to the sea. Keep going until you reach a wooden boardwalk extending onto the beach **B** and turn in towards the village. Walk through to a street, turning right and then left to reach a junction opposite a green and boathouse at the foot of The Meare.

Follow the main street to the right, hugging a verge beside the lake and continuing past a drive to the golf club. Just beyond there, turn left along a track on the left, Uplands Road, which takes you to the House in the Clouds and Thorpeness Windmill **C**.

> The two most eye-catching buildings in the village are the **windmill** and **House in the Clouds**. Originally built in Aldringham to grind corn, the 19th-century mill was brought to Thorpeness in 1923 to pump water from a well into a storage tank perched high on a tower opposite. The tower was later boxed in to create what must be one of the strangest houses in the country.

Return to the main street and continue left to a junction in front of the almshouses. Go right to pass The Dolphin and then, approaching a bend, turn off onto the first of a pair of adjacent tracks leaving on

The Meare

The House in the Clouds

the left in front of a thatched barn. Follow it up to some houses and curve around with it to the right. Just a little farther on, bear left and then right at successive forks onto a broad track signed as a byway **D**. Climbing gently, follow the track

> **?** When were the almshouses at Thorpeness built?

for almost ¼ mile (400m) at the edge of gorse and bramble heath. Eventually, as it begins to swing right, look for a narrower path forking off through the thicket on the left, just before the entrance to a field. The path initially runs

between hedges that curve above to become almost tunnel-like in places, before emerging once again onto more open heath.

Where the path then splits **E**, take the right-hand branch and walk on to meet a lateral track. Go right and immediately left to find a stile into the Aldringham Walks Conservation Area, from which a waymarked path winds on across the heath. Emerging at the far side into the corner of a field given over to the husbandry of pigs, go right and walk at the edge of rough ground beside the nature reserve's perimeter fence. When you later

Post mill in Thorpeness

reach a junction of tracks, keep ahead, passing between field entrances on either side to continue on a hedged track. It later broadens before ending at a tarmac drive by a thatched cottage **F**.

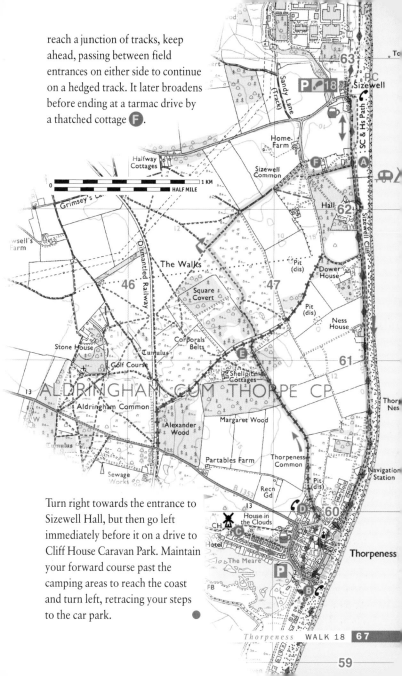

Turn right towards the entrance to Sizewell Hall, but then go left immediately before it on a drive to Cliff House Caravan Park. Maintain your forward course past the camping areas to reach the coast and turn left, retracing your steps to the car park.

19 *Burnham Thorpe*

START Burnham Thorpe
(grid ref: TF 851417)
DISTANCE 5½ miles
(8.8km)
TIME 2½ hours
PARKING Parking area on
north side of Burnham
Thorpe's church
ROUTE FEATURES Field
paths and quiet lanes

This quiet corner of Norfolk is proud to have produced England's most famous admiral, Horatio Nelson. His father was parson of the church at Burnham Thorpe and, although the house in which he spent his early years no longer stands, the young lad must have trodden the very same paths followed on this walk when he wandered down to the sea to watch coastal traders and fishing boats berthing in the creek.

From the grass car park behind All Saints Church, go right to the corner of the lane where, on the left, you will find a kissing-gate into the corner of a field. Follow the right-hand field edge away, passing into the next field by a reed-filled pond. The water is in fact part of the River Burn, and will be encountered again during the walk, when it passes in full flow beneath Burnham Overy Mill. A trod diverging from the boundary guides your onward steps across an expanse of rough grazing. Crossing a plank bridge over a drain in the middle, keep going to the distant corner where another kissing-gate takes you out onto the overgrown embankment of a disused railway line **A**.

Go left, but after 100 yds (91m), look for a path dropping off on the right. Walk through the tree belt below to break out onto the edge of pasture. Follow the boundary away to the right and continue at the edge of the subsequent field to emerge onto a lane at Burnham Overy Town **B**. Go right past a row of cottages, at the end of

PUBLIC TRANSPORT None
REFRESHMENTS The Nelson in Burnham Thorpe and The Hero at Burnham Overy
Staithe, where the seafront chandlery also serves drinks and snacks
PUBLIC TOILETS None
ORDNANCE SURVEY MAPS Explorer 251 (Norfolk Coast Central)

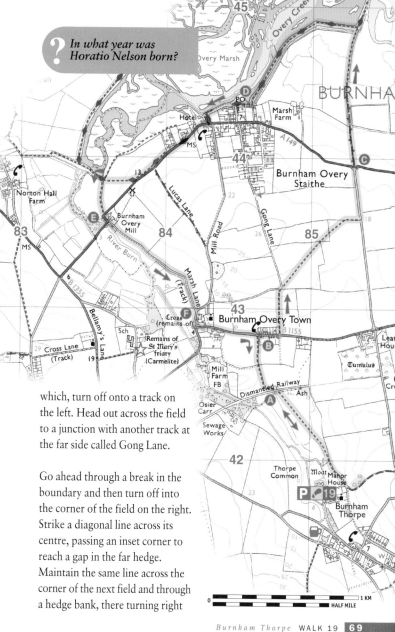

In what year was Horatio Nelson born?

which, turn off onto a track on the left. Head out across the field to a junction with another track at the far side called Gong Lane.

Go ahead through a break in the boundary and then turn off into the corner of the field on the right. Strike a diagonal line across its centre, passing an inset corner to reach a gap in the far hedge. Maintain the same line across the corner of the next field and through a hedge bank, there turning right

Burnham Overy watermill

Born the sixth child of a humble country parson, **Horatio Nelson** first went to sea at the age of 12. Although captain by the age of 21, the real turning point in his career was his victory over the French at the Battle of the Nile in 1798. In 1805 he sent his famous signal 'England expects that every man will do his duty' as his fleet sailed into the Battle of Trafalgar. His strategy won the day, but Nelson was shot as the engagement ended. His body was brought back home in a cask of rum and interred in St Paul's, though it is at his family church in Burnham Thorpe that he is most warmly remembered.

to walk beside it. Breaking out onto a lane, walk left down to the main road **C**.

Look out for traffic as you cross to a track opposite, which heads out over the marshes towards the distant sea defences. This section of the coast is protected as a National Nature Reserve, a stile part way along the track taking you across its boundary. Through a gate at the far end, climb onto the broad embankment and follow it left above Overy Creek to the old landing of Burnham Overy Staithe **D**.

Reaching the tiny hamlet, join the road to continue along the waterfront. One of the cottages around the corner was the home of Captain Richard Woodget, master of the Cutty Sark. The famous three-masted clipper was launched in 1869 and served the south sea trades, first bringing tea from China and later transporting wool produced on the vast Australian sheep farms. But, by that time, the age of steam was already well established, and she was one of the last great sailing vessels to be built. However, her turn of speed ensured that the Cutty Sark continued trading well into the 20th century before retiring as a training ship. The famous vessel now lies fully restored in a dry dock at Greenwich.

Turning away at the far end of the harbour, the street leads back to the main road. Walk right to leave the village, abandoning the road when you reach the end of the pavement through a gap in the hedge on the right. A parallel path continues at the field edge until, approaching a windmill set back on the other side of the road, it veers across the field to an earthen flood embankment at the far side. Crossing over the bank, drop left to a stile beside a gate and walk away alongside the hedge towards the road.

Emerging by a picturesque pond below Burnham Overy Mill **E**, walk forward towards it. Cross the lane on the bend and keep ahead between the mill buildings and through a yard to a gate at the back. Carry on along the edge of a riverside meadow, passing through a gate in the corner beside a group of

pollarded willows to continue on a hedged track, Marsh Lane. It finishes on the outskirts of the village of Burnham Overy Town **F**.

Turn right along the lane to a junction, a stone standing on a tiny green marking the spot where merchants used to clinch their deals. The stone was sometimes called a nail, and is the derivation of the expression 'paying on the nail'. Go left, passing the entrance to St Clement's Church, which has a rather unusual internal arrangement, as you will discover if you venture inside. Beyond, the lane runs between fields, shortly approaching some more cottages by a red telephone box. Meeting your outward route **B**, turn into the field on the right and retrace your steps back to Burnham Thorpe Church. ●

Cottages in Burnham Overy Staithe

20 Hickling Broad and Potter Heigham

START Potter Heigham (grid ref: TG 420184)
DISTANCE 6 miles (9.7km)
TIME 2½ hours
PARKING Car park at Potter Heigham (Pay and Display)
ROUTE FEATURES Field and woodland paths and tracks

Boat owners could be forgiven for believing that the only way to appreciate the Norfolk Broads is from the water, but there is a great deal to enjoy on the marshes and in the woods that surround them. This longer but easy walk explores the fringes of the largest expanse of open water, Hickling Broad, revealing the tremendous diversity of the surrounding countryside.

Joining the road at the car park entrance, follow it over Heigham Bridge, leaving immediately beyond on the right onto a broad grass verge beside the river. Walk upstream beneath a modern bridge carrying the main road and continue along a surfaced path beside a line of holiday chalets. Do not be put off by this unappealing beginning to the walk, for in time the last of them is passed. The path dog-legs around a ditch emanating from a drainage mill and continues beside the reeds bordering the River Thurne. Surprisingly, despite its distance from the sea, the river is still tidal at this point, and indeed remains so to almost its end, the ebb and flow of the subtly changing water levels determining when the pumps of the drains feeding it spring into action. Keep going, eventually passing a boathouse on the opposite bank before the path kicks away from the river to follow Candle Dyke towards Hickling Broad **A**.

Approaching the mouth of the

PUBLIC TRANSPORT Bus service to Potter Heigham
REFRESHMENTS The Broadshaven Tavern, café and fish and chip shop at Potter Heigham
PUBLIC TOILETS At Potter Heigham
ORDNANCE SURVEY MAPS Explorer OL40 (The Broads)

Candle Dyke

broad is an eel fishery, where nets are strung from bank to bank beneath the water. The way then leaves the water's edge to continue on an elevated path through the reed beds enclosing the foot of the lake. Later passing into scrub, keep going to eventually reach a stile and continue at the edge of a wood. Predominantly of oak, birch and alder, the woodland adds another dimension to the landscape and encourages a great many songbirds, more often heard than seen. Warm sunny days bring out an abundance of another of the area's inhabitants, the dragonfly. So much an integral part of the environment, the rare 'Norfolk hawker', which is only found on the Broads, has been adopted by the Broads National Park as its emblem. A broad ditch separates you from the wood, whilst beyond the reeds on the right, the open

The name of the village remembers a **Roman pottery** producing bricks and funeral urns that occupied a nearby hill (a relative term in this part of the country). That the trade continued into the Middle Ages is reflected in the unusual 15th-century font in **St Nicholas's Church**, which is constructed of bricks and tiles. Today the village is one of the 'capitals' of the Broads holiday and boat trades, despite its 14th-century bridge being a paint-scraping challenge for many boat owners.

water of the lake is never far away. It is suddenly revealed in a clearing where there is a small landing stage, and again a little later on where a bird hide provides a commanding view **B**.

Over a stile beyond the hide, the path, resuming briefly at the edge of more woodland, leads over another stile and on to a junction. Turn left across a footbridge into the trees, wandering through to a stile at the far side **C**. *There is now a choice of return routes, each about the same length but offering different views across the countryside. One takes you past the lovely church of St Nicholas, whilst*

Beside Hickling Broad

the other winds across the fields, where we discovered a slow worm basking in the sun upon the path. Why it is called a slow worm is hard to imagine, as once startled, it disappeared with an amazing turn of speed!

To go back by way of the church, turn right and then left to follow a track away across the fields. Swinging right at the far side, emerge onto the corner of a lane and walk left to reach the church **D**. A charming building from the outside, there is much of beauty to see inside, although if locked you will first have to borrow the key. Details of the key holders are posted within the porch, but to avoid an additional walk, should you find it shut, it might be preferable to return later in the car. The walk continues left along Marsh Road to meet a track at its very end. Turn right, joining the alternative route coming from the left **E**.

*If you elect to return across the fields from point **C**, turn left, shortly leaving the trees behind to continue between open fields. Reaching a crossing track, go ahead over a plank bridge and carry on at the edge of a copse. In a little distance developing as a track, the way continues ahead, before long*

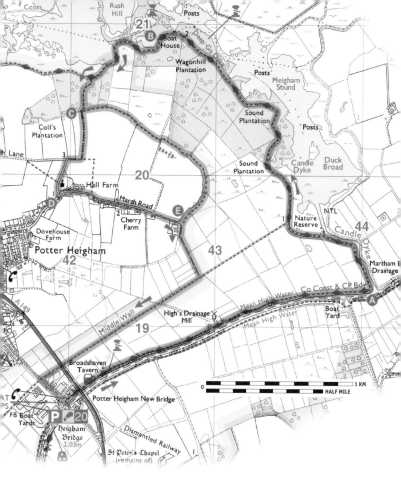

passing a junction where Marsh Road joins from the right E.

Carry on to another junction and there turn right onto a long straight track, crossing the marshland grazing to reach the main road. *Take care crossing as the traffic moves quickly*, and continue along

> **How old is Heigham Bridge?**

another track opposite. It finally brings you out onto the road near Heigham Bridge. The car park from which the walk began lies a short distance to the left. ●

Further Information

Walking Safety

Always take with you both warm and waterproof clothing and sufficient food and drink. Wear suitable footwear, such as strong walking boots or shoes that give a good grip over stony ground, on slippery slopes and in muddy conditions. Try to obtain a local weather forecast and bear it in mind before you start. Do not be afraid to abandon your proposed route and return to your starting point in the event of a sudden and unexpected deterioration in the weather.

All the walks described in this book will be safe to do, given due care and respect, even during the winter. Indeed, a crisp, fine winter day often provides perfect walking conditions, with firm ground underfoot and a clarity of light unique to that time of the year.

The most difficult hazard likely to be encountered is mud, especially when walking along woodland and field paths, farm tracks and bridleways – the latter in particular can often get churned up by cyclists and horses. In summer, an additional difficulty may be narrow and overgrown paths, particularly along the edges of cultivated fields. Neither should constitute a major problem provided that the appropriate footwear is worn.

Follow the Country Code

- Enjoy the countryside and respect its life and work
- Guard against all risk of fire
- Take your litter home
- Fasten all gates
- Help to keep all water clean
- Keep your dogs under control
- Protect wildlife, plants and trees
- Keep to public paths across farmland
- Take special care on country roads
- Leave livestock, crops and machinery alone
- Make no unnecessary noise
- Use gates and stiles to cross fences, hedges and walls
            (The Countryside Agency)

Useful Organisations

The Broads Authority – a member of the family of National Parks
18 Colegate,
Norwich
NR3 1BQ
Tel. 01603 610734
www.broads-authority.gov.uk

The viewpoint on Stone Hill

Camping and Caravanning Club
Greenfields House, Westwood
Way, Coventry CV4 8JH
Tel. 024 7669 4995
www.campingandcaravanningclub.
co.uk

**Council for the Protection of Rural
England**
128 Southwark Street,
London SE1 0SW
Tel. 020 7981 2800
www.cpre.org.uk

Countryside Agency
John Dower House,
Crescent Place, Cheltenham
GL50 3RA
Tel. 01242 521381
www.countryside.gov.uk

English Heritage
Customer Services Department,
PO Box 569, Swindon
SN2 2YP
Tel. 0870 333 1181
www.english-heritage.org.uk

Dragonflies are numerous on the Broads

English Nature
Northminster House,
Peterborough PE1 1UA
Tel. 01733 455101
www.english-nature.org.uk

National Trust
Membership and general enquiries:
PO Box 39, Warrington
WA5 7WD
Tel. 0870 458 4000
www.nationaltrust.org.uk

National Trust East of England
Regional Office
Tel. 0870 609 5388

Norfolk County Council
County Hall, Martineau Lane,
Norwich NR1 2DH
Tel. 01603 223284

Norfolk Wildlife Trust
Bewick House,
22 Thorpe Road,
Norwich NR1 1RY
Tel. 01603 625540
www.wildlifetrust.org.uk/norfolk

Norfolk Windmills Trust
County Hall, Martineau Lane,
Norwich NR1 2SG
Tel. 01603 222705
www.norfolkwindmills.co.uk

Ordnance Survey
Romsey Road, Maybush,
Southampton SO16 4GU
Tel. 08456 050505 (Lo-call)

Ramblers' Association
2nd Floor, Camelford House,
87-90 Albert Embankment,